'Rupert Shortt shows that Richard Dawkins's attacks on theism rest on an almost total misunderstanding of what theists actually believe. He shows that God is not understood by religious believers as just another being in the universe, but as the sustaining power on which the universe depends. Dawkins's refusal to read any serious theology means that he has no idea what he is talking about.'
John Barton, Formerly Oriel and Laing Professor of the Interpretation of Holy Scripture, University of Oxford; author of *A History of the Bible: The Book and its Faiths*

'Rupert Shortt's counter-argument to Richard Dawkins's latest patronising attack on religious believers is aimed with killer accuracy at weaknesses in Dawkins's case. It is also brisk, learned, and very readable. It deserves to be read by both the convinced and waverers in each camp.'
Lucy Beckett, writer; author of *In the Light of Christ: Writings in the Western Tradition*

'Rupert Shortt draws on rich intellectual resources in the Socratic tradition, all the more persuasively as he is not a religious office-holder, to show that dogmatic atheism is based on an insecure concept of science.'
Jonathan Benthall, Director Emeritus, Royal Anthropological Institute; author of *Returning to Religion: Why a Secular Age is Haunted by Faith*

'It is well past the moment when childish atheists like Dawkins and the religious fundamentalists they at once despise and mimic should have been consigned together to one of culture's obscurer nurseries and left to fling their toys at one another until nap-time overtakes them. Shortt's brief, keen-edged, militantly rational book is a splendid reminder of how adults discuss matters of ultimate importance.'
David Bentley Hart, former Templeton Fellow, University of Notre Dame Institute for Advanced Study; author of *Atheist Delusions: The Christian Revolution and its Fashionable Enemies*

'In this richly documented and highly readable essay Rupert Shortt deftly demonstrates just how often Richard Dawkins's most recent broadside against religion simply miss-es the target.'
John Cottingham, Professor of Philosophy of Religion, University of Roehampton; author of *The Spiritual Dimension: Religion, Philosophy and Human Value*

'Thank God for Rupert Shortt. His clarity penetrates depths. His concision cuts through cant. His fairness exposes arrogance and narrow-mindedness. He helps us see the toughness, subtlety, and complexity of a rationally approachable yet intensely experi-enced God. By comparison, atheism, though reasonable and respectable, seems intel-lectually shallow and cognitively deficient.'
Felipe Fernández-Armesto, P   ıe; author of
Out of Our Minds: What We

'Rupert Shortt criticises Dawkins's dogmatic atheism, demonstrating that it is based on superficial arguments against religious belief, which he hasn't understood. This is a clearly written and fair-minded demolition of Dawkins's shallow thinking on religious belief.'
Keith R. Fox, Associate Director, The Faraday Institute for Science and Religion; editor of *Drug-DNA Interaction Protocols*

'A bracing demonstration that a Christian can myth-bust an atheist quite as effectively as vice versa.'
Tom Holland, historian and broadcaster; author of *Dominion: The Making of the Western Mind*

'This is a great read. Rupert Shortt demolishes Richard Dawkins's argument with consummate elegance. As Shortt sees it, Dawkins is the child and those who take a more measured, intellectually exploratory approach, are the grown-ups. Dawkins's arrogant tone is exposed as the approach of the convinced atheist, who lacks substantive and evidence-based arguments to support his conviction. Now it's time for Richard Dawkins to read and digest it, so that he can understand that his childhood exposure to Protestant Christianity is not all there is to theology.'
Julia Neuberger DBE, Senior Rabbi of the West London Synagogue; author of *Is That All There Is? Thoughts on the Meaning of Life and Leaving a Legacy*

'No one is better placed than Rupert Shortt to provide a just, nuanced and readable response to the anti-religion industry that is Richard Dawkins. Rich with references to the scientists, philosophers and theologians Dawkins chooses to ignore, the book will be a welcome read for many who seek a concise survey of this debate.'
Janet Soskice, Professor of Philosophical Theology, University of Cambridge; editor of *Creation 'Ex Nihilo' and Modern Theology*

Outgrowing Dawkins confirms Rupert Shortt's reputation as one of the people you head straight to for a thoughtful, honest and engaging defence of *mature* Christianity. A little gem.
Nick Spencer, Senior Fellow, Theos; author of *Darwin and God*

'Rupert Shortt's pithy responses are thoughtful, eloquent and thought-provoking. He is well-informed about the scientific issues, expert in the philosophy of religion, and balanced overall in his judgements of where we are and what a fair and honest education would look like in the contemporary world. A refreshing, cultured, and at times gently humourous companion, but most of all cogent and pertinent to our day.'
Andrew Steane, Professor of Physics, University of Oxford; author of *Science and Humanity: A Humane Philosophy of Science and Religion*

'An elegant and timely reminder that religious belief is rational and sane, and that it is not refuted by science.'
A. N. Wilson, writer and broadcaster; author of *The Book of the People: How to Read the Bible*

Rupert Shortt is religion editor of *The Times Literary Supplement* and a Research Associate at the University of Cambridge. His books include *Benedict XVI* (2005), *Christianophobia: A Faith under Attack* (2012), *Rowan's Rule: The Biography of the Archbishop* (2014), *God Is No Thing: Coherent Christianity* (2016) and *Does Religion Do More Harm Than Good?* (2019).

OUTGROWING DAWKINS

God for Grown-Ups

RUPERT SHORTT

First published in Great Britain in 2019

Society for Promoting Christian Knowledge
36 Causton Street
London SW1P 4ST
www.spck.org.uk

British Library Cataloguing-in-Publication Data
A catalogue record for this book is available from the British Library

ISBN 978–0–281–08410–4
eBook ISBN 978–0–281–08411–p1

1 3 5 7 9 10 8 6 4 2

Typeset by The Book Guild Ltd, Leicester, UK
Printed in Great Britain by Jellyfish Print Solutions

eBook by The Book Guild Ltd, Leicester, UK

Produced on paper from sustainable forests

For Alison Shell and Arnold Hunt

When we speak of God we do not clear up a puzzle; we draw attention to a mystery.
Herbert McCabe

If God is source of all, holding everything – including time and space themselves – in being, then it follows that you cannot think of God as one more item in the universe, as one outsized actor among others, as vying for space or influence with the beings God creates.
Karen Kilby

The aim of God's creation is that creation should help make itself, and the Scriptures are humanly written and developed history riddled with ambiguities and dead-ends and fresh starts. Nevertheless, they are powerfully challenging calls to humanity to grow and reform and criticise itself.
Timothy McDermott

Honest doubts are by definition better than false certainties – no prizes there: but who says science has the one and religion the other? I can think of certain dogmas of materialist science, just as I can of religious dogmas, that are false certainties that impede its access to truth; equally the exploratory process involved in an openness to the idea of God raises as many questions as it answers, just as does the genuinely exploratory process of true science. There is scientistic fundamentalism and there is religious fundamentalism: why waste time on either?
Iain McGilchrist

Now, even though the realms of religion and science in themselves are clearly marked off from each other, nevertheless there exist between the two strong reciprocal relationships and dependencies... Science without religion is lame, religion without science is blind.
Albert Einstein

For many religious practitioners ... devotional and contemplative practices are ways to reach towards the transcendent, and possibly even touch it. Over time, these practices open up their minds and bodies, expand their receptivity, shift the horizon of what they can feel and understand. And after years of practice it may no longer seem strange or unnatural to perceive moments of grace, when the transcendent flows right through the middle of life.
Clare Carlisle

Contents

Preface

My remit in this very brief book is tight. It does not provide point-by-point critical commentary on *Outgrowing God*. Several comprehensive rebuttals of *The God Delusion*, Richard Dawkins's more detailed polemic, have already appeared. Nor do I offer a survey of the toxic religion that still forms one of atheism's principal assets. I take the menace posed by spiritual fanaticism for granted – and have discussed it in detail elsewhere. In what follows I simply turn the soil at some significant points in a large field, to show that some of Professor Dawkins's main claims look far less credible from the standpoint of a mature faith. If you start by assuming that religion entails an abusive relationship with a Zeus-like figure who idly makes imperfect toys – and tortures them for their imperfections if they don't adore him in return – you are missing something fundamental. As I indicate, it is as crude as dismissing all left-wing thought and endeavour as marks of communism, or all conservatism as fascistic. That such bigotry prospers in these polarized times forms a further reason for calling it out.

The approach is bottom-up not top-down, partly because of a perceived need to broaden the discussion. Though *Outgrowing God* trains most of its fire on Christianity, it seems to me important to consider the religious cast of mind more generally, even if only in outline. I have therefore restated in a simplified form some of the arguments from my earlier books *God is No Thing* and *Does Religion Do More Harm Than Good?*. Gaps inevitably remain: those wishing to navigate the landscape with a full set of equipment will find more detailed resources in the works listed at the end.

For the invitation to write *Outgrowing Dawkins*, I am very grateful to Philip Law and his colleagues at SPCK. Their encouragement has meant a great deal. I am also highly indebted to some distinguished scientists for discussing themes in their specialist areas with me: the physiologist Denis Noble, the physicist Andrew Steane, the cosmologist Marc Manera, the biochemist Keith Fox, and the geneticist Denis Alexander. A cluster of philosophers and theologians have fed my thinking over a longer period, notably Sarah Coakley, John Cottingham, Tim Crane, Anthony Kenny, Janet Soskice and Vernon White.

In an atomized intellectual culture, praise is also due to figures who straddle the worlds of science and theology. Few do so with as much skill as Andrew Davison. His kindness and rigour have inspired many besides me.

For guidance and other forms of support, I am also profoundly thankful to Stig Abell, Ella Baron, Lucy Beckett, Madeline Cohen, Richard Conrad OP, Brian Griffiths, Bernice Martin, Maren Meinhardt, José Prado, Alvin Uzcanga and David Warnes.

Rupert Shortt
London

1

A dialogue of the deaf

I recently met an old friend at a party. She works for a Christian NGO. Later that evening we were introduced to a man with a background in software engineering. Having learnt about my friend's job and then discovered that she goes to church, he asked her how old she thought the universe is. Her jaw dropped a bit. But she was composed enough to reply with a counter-question. 'Did you know that it was a Catholic priest [the cosmologist Georges LeMaître] who proposed the Big Bang theory in the first place?' Now it was the engineer's turn to look shocked.

Some may dismiss this exchange as a flash in the pan. To others it will reflect a dialogue of the deaf evident across Western culture and beyond. The frustration felt by this second group is well founded in my view. Popular contemporary attitudes towards religion include condescending dismissal. The same applies to large sections of the media, universities and the arts establishment.[1] Faith groups must bear their share of the blame for this. But so must the strident atheists who reject what they have never taken the trouble to investigate beyond a superficial level – especially those who write bestsellers ridiculing belief systems they know so little about.

How might scientifically informed religious believers defend the coherence of their world view? If they are Christians, say, part of their answer might derive from the words of Timothy McDermott, theologian and professor of computer science, quoted at the outset of this book. 'The aim of God's creation is that creation should help make itself, and the Scriptures are humanly written and developed history riddled with ambiguities and dead-ends and fresh starts. Nevertheless, they are powerfully challenging calls to humanity to grow and reform and criticize itself.' This sort of judgement could be voiced in allied ways across the spiritual spectrum. 'We have a deep respect for science,' people of various stripes often add. 'We just don't think that this way of investigating the world exhausts all reality.'

In particular, there is no contradiction between accepting Darwin's theories and belief in God. Young-earth creationists and advocates of intelligent design are therefore mistaken. So, too, are those who assume an unbridgeable divide between science and religion.

Four reasons especially might be cited in favour of such a model. The first is intellectual. Honest enquirers should follow the evidence where it leads, whether or not they practise a faith. There is nothing pious or wishful about this: a pillar of Christian orthodoxy such as St Thomas Aquinas would have insisted on the 'unitary' character of truth. If science establishes that water boils at 100 degrees Celsius or that the world is 13.7 billion years old, then these and other discoveries cannot be credibly challenged from any pulpit.

The second is theological. Classical teaching in various traditions, Eastern as well as Western, represents God not as a big thing competing for space with lesser things, but as the *ground* of existence. One useful analogy is that of the author in relation to his or her characters. While not himself a cast member of *War and Peace*, Tolstoy nevertheless inhabits every line of the narrative. Another analogy is supplied by light. The light in which we see is not one of the objects seen, because we see light only inasmuch as it is reflected off opaque objects. Nature has its own integrity according to laws and patterns established by science. To repeat: God is not a micro-manager intervening here and there. Nor is the relationship between God and the world like that of a builder to a house. Things are both subtler and more intimate from a monotheistic standpoint. As a canvas supports a painting or a singer holds a song, God sustains everything in being moment by moment. We are talking about a deeper level of causation. So when someone turns on the gas to heat up a pan of water, for example, chemistry can give a full account in its own terms of the process involved. But a Hindu or Muslim or Jew or Christian can still maintain that God makes the whole situation exist: the gas, its power and its action on the water. God and the gas work at different levels, not in competition.

Divine being is also seen as unfathomable in the major faiths. 'God may be loved, but not thought,' as a classic such as *The Cloud of Unknowing* puts it. 'By love may he be gotten and holden; but by thought never.' Believers can nonetheless combine humility in the face of a profound mystery with a calm certainty about what God is not. In the case of a figure like Richard Dawkins, by contrast, things are turned upside down. Starting with an utterly inadequate definition of God as an angry tyrant in the sky, he then informs us that this monster doesn't exist. It's a true belief widely shared by people on either side of the religious divide. But why should it necessarily be an argument for atheism rather than a spur to resist idolatry?

Initial mistakes breed larger ones when unchecked. If I say that my favourite drink is beer and you reply that yours is wine, we are at least agreed on what it is we disagree about. But since the deity in whom Dawkins disbelieves is a blown-up creature, he has even gone on to make the surreal claim that our supposed creator would need to have evolved through natural selection, and there is no available evidence of any life form more sophisticated than humankind. In other words, 'God' is being pictured as both the cause of the universe and a product of it. Fallacies rarely come larger than this.[2]

Our third reason is textual. Let us focus on the Christian narrative for now, since it has prompted so much derision in English-speaking circles. Are those

7

who take the first chapters of Genesis literally (some atheists, as well as creationists, as we have seen) reading the Bible in an appropriate way? Countless mainstream voices would say no. The essential message of Genesis is that God has invited the world into being, but that from the start things have gone seriously wrong with humanity. Despite this, however, God has not given up on us. We will only contrast 'good' modern science with the 'bad' kind found in scripture if we make the category mistake of reading Genesis as a biological textbook. A common tactic employed by sceptics involves showing how fundamentalist interpretations of the creation story in Genesis 2, or the Genesis 9 flood narrative, are incompatible with their scientific account. So far so good – though a bit easy and contemptuous. These pundits then identify the biblical picture with a fundamentalist interpretation. That shows a lamentable surrender to the fundamentalist mode of thought, which any self-respecting scientist should know how to resist.[3]

Yes, many believers did read Genesis simplistically before the modern era (though by no means all: St Augustine, perhaps the most influential thinker in Christian history, argued in the fourth century that since the Sun and Moon were not created till the fourth 'day', the creation story was better understood figuratively). But orthodox Christianity does not hold the Bible to be factually inerrant. Scripture itself nowhere claims such a status. Prizing a text – believing that it discloses the truth of our condition with unique richness – is not the same as holding every word of it to be infallible. And the Protestant fundamentalism on which the New Atheists rely for plausibility is a new kid on the block in historical terms, owing much to culture wars in the United States.

The fourth reason is historical. The myth that science and religion are and always have been in conflict is vital to sustain trench warfare between the two polarized forces already referred to – creationists and supporters of intelligent design on the one hand and, on the other, those who dismiss all religion as fundamentally irrational. Yet Copernicus, Galileo, Descartes, Newton, Leibniz, Michael Faraday, James Clerk Maxwell and other builders of the modern world were men of deep religious conviction as well as scientific geniuses. What's more, their work was preceded by that of medieval pioneers – Muslims and Jews, as well as Christians – often working in productive dialogue. Of course there has been tension between science and theology at times, a classic example being the Oxford debate between T. H. Huxley and Samuel Wilberforce in 1860 (although much of the reporting of this encounter is skewed). Take a broader view, however, and you may be struck by how flexible many Christians and others have been in absorbing new knowledge.

As is often noted, before castigating Galileo – a process more due to the clash of confrontational individuals than to scientific matters per se – the Catholic Church jettisoned biblical cosmology in favour of a Greek model, based on the movement of the spheres. Understanding the geological record and its implications for biblical timelines was a task undertaken within a predominantly Christian culture. Francis Spufford makes the point with characteristic verve: 'there's a good case to be made that the ready acceptance of evolution in Britain owed a lot to the great cultural transmission mechanism of the Church of England. If you're glad that Darwin is on the £10 note, hug an Anglican.'[4]

Among scholars of this field, it is widely accepted that two works in particular encapsulate the warfare narrative: John William Draper's *History of the Conflict between Religion and Science* (1875) and Andrew Dickson White's *A History of the Warfare of Science with Theology in Christendom* (1896). No professional historian now takes these works seriously. Though many of the 'facts' listed in these books were made up, the damage they caused endures. As the biologist Denis Alexander has observed, researchers are still correcting the 'factual mutants'[5] created by Draper and Dickson White.

A much more objective survey of the terrain can be found in *Galileo Goes to Jail: And other Myths About Science and Religion,*[6] edited by Ronald Numbers. Amid much else, this book shows that multiple features of contemporary science were nurtured in theological soil, among them trust in the intelligibility of the world, the concept of physical laws, and empiricism itself. The founders of the Royal Society in seventeenth-century England wrote of how their Christian faith impelled them to explore their surroundings. The father of natural history, John Ray, was a Puritan. Christians in the twentieth century such as the Anglican R. A. Fisher and the Orthodox Theodosius Dobzhansky did much to develop the neo-Darwinian consensus. In our own day it is not just figures of no religious allegiance, but also Martin Novak, a Harvard-based Catholic, and Simon Conway Morris, another Anglican, who are contributing significantly to evolutionary theory.

One obvious corollary of all this is that a substantial portion of recent public discourse – especially in Europe and North America – is redundant. I refer of course to New Atheism and especially to its best-known exponents, nicknamed the Four Horsemen.[7] Dawkins, author of *The God Delusion* and now of *Outgrowing God: A Beginner's Guide to Atheism*,[8] is perhaps this posse's most dogged member. Adjacent furrows on the same patch have been ploughed by the late Christopher Hitchens in *God Is Not Great*,[9] Sam Harris in *The End of Faith*[10] and Daniel Dennett in *Breaking the Spell*.[11] Stephen Fry, one of their foremost celebrity cheerleaders, has also likened them to the Four Musketeers.[12] The martial language is apt. These men are able gunslingers and sword-wielders, but far less proficient with scalpels.

Don't take my word for it alone. Since church teaching (or rather wholesale travesties of it) is made to do duty for religion in general throughout *The*

God Delusion, the book has drawn full-scale rebuttals from Christian writers. The former atheist and biochemist-turned-theologian Alister McGrath employed a steady hand in *The Dawkins Delusion?*[13] David Bentley Hart opted for lethal force in *Atheist Delusions*.[14] So did Edward Feser in *The Last Superstition*.[15] The philosopher Denys Turner has protested that 'there is scarcely a proposition of [St Thomas Aquinas's] theology that Dawkins is able to formulate accurately enough to succeed in accurately denying'.[16]

Maybe most notable of all is the hostility Dawkins has prompted among his fellow non-believers. Terry Eagleton, critic and literary theorist, famously began his review of *The God Delusion* in the *London Review of Books* as follows: 'Imagine someone holding forth on biology whose only knowledge of the subject is the *British Book of Birds*, and you have a rough idea of what it feels like to read Richard Dawkins on theology'.[17] Anthony Kenny, one of the world's most distinguished agnostic thinkers, has described Dawkins's writings on religion as marked by 'tendentious paraphrase, imputation of bad faith, outright insult'.[18] Kenny was himself once a priest before losing his faith and becoming an academic. Another renowned philosopher, John Gray, has never held religious beliefs of any kind. Yet his book *Seven Kinds of Atheism*[19] is especially critical of Dawkins for displaying the same provinciality of mind as the most stiff-necked believer. You will find more insight into the subject of faith in the opening few pages of this excellent book than in either of Dawkins's screeds in their entirety.

Consider, too, a major article by Giovanni Tiso published in the Summer 2019 issue of *New Humanist* magazine[20] on the failure of New Atheism. The piece is significant in drawing attention to the movement's wider cultural ramifications, not just its unfocused grasp of its targets. Tiso condemns the Horsemen's shared tone as 'a mix of assured belligerence and petulant self-regard'. Their bid to establish their own status as truth-seekers is hollow, because it involves laying waste to 'a largely imaginary opponent'. They go on, Tiso adds wryly, to ask how any person of faith should suppose *them* to be arrogant and shrill, when it is all the fault of believers for swallowing such naïve creeds in the first place.

He is happy to let the Four do his work for him simply by quoting them:

'The thing about religious people is that they recite the Nicene Creed every week,' says Dawkins, rhetorically converting everyone to Christianity, 'and yet they have the gall to accuse us of being overconfident.' Dennett echoes: 'The religions have contrived to make it impossible to disagree with them critically without being rude.' To which Harris responds: 'Our criticism is actually more barbed than that. We're not merely offending people, we're also telling them that they're wrong to be offended.' Dennett again: 'And there there's no polite way to say to somebody...' Harris completes the sentence, cheerfully: '"You've wasted your life!"'[21]

Tiso's verdict also speaks for itself. 'These, remember, are four adults incredulous that people call them arrogant.'

Again: insofar as Dawkins, Dennett, Harris and Hitchens oppose superstition, narrow-mindedness and hostility to science, then their complaints are of course welcome if hardly new. But any virtues in their writings on faith are deflected by the vices of distortion and intellectual imperialism. As suggested, the distortions lie in taking the weakest possible statements of the case for belief and ridiculing them as though they were the only versions going. To win a serious argument as opposed to a shouting match, you need the honesty and grit to engage with a robust version of your opponent's case. The imperialism derives from too sparse an account of human reason.

Outgrowing God is fluently written and a salute to biology, as well as a blunt statement of the case for atheism. Myth-making darkness – the subject of the opening chapters – gives way in later sections to scientific light. There is an admirable account of today's scientific consensus on how the biosphere evolved. Readers are then invited to be proud of it, to pity poor myth-makers, scorn creationists and scratch their heads over the inadequate rationality of non-atheists. Firm direction is given on where to applaud and where to snigger. And here, sadly, is the reason why Dawkins's latest book cannot be recommended to beginners or anyone else – other than as an object lesson in the perils of trashing what you don't understand.

It is pitched at a younger audience in the register of Ernst Gombrich's *A Little History of the World*. Among the virtues of that classic is its objectivity. Dawkins consistently mars a good scientific story with spin. His conclusions are so callow overall that they can be summed up as resting on a single dodgy syllogism:

Major premise: Evolution by natural selection is incompatible with belief in a creator God.
Minor premise: Evolution by natural selection is true.
'Conclusion': Belief in a creator God is false.

Aside from reaffirming their acceptance of Darwin's theories and thus denying Dawkins's major premise, there are many other things people of faith might want to say in response. One is that their convictions cannot be separated from the personal commitment supplying an overarching context to their lives. In other words, they haven't thought their way into a new way of living, but lived their way into a new way of thinking. This is hardly to imply soft-headedness. Many who share this outlook supplement it with a muscular claim that belief in God is a valid inference of philosophical reflection. In other words, the world is not self-created. Existence is on loan from a source. (The philosophical stance known as naturalism entails a confidence that everything can ultimately be explained in the language of natural science. But it is not possible, in the terms naturalism allows, to say how anything at all can exist.) They may amplify their vision by drawing on a maxim of the philosopher Eugene Gendlin: 'We think more than we can say. We feel more than we can think. We live more than we can feel. And there is much else besides.' In a similar way, believers might add, perceiving God's presence is a far cry from knowing what God is. Note the expansive understanding of a word such as 'reasonable' here. To develop our earlier observation, the thoughtful Muslim or Jew or Hindu or Christian is essentially saying, 'Although faith cannot or should not contradict science, there are all sorts of statements, starting with ethics, that I hold true but which cannot be demonstrated in a test tube. It isn't reasonable to think that only reason *defined in one narrow way* discloses the world to us. The grain of reality is revealed by a combination of reason and our moral and aesthetic impulses. This is the context in which spiritual belief may enter the picture.'

Simply stated, Dawkins's doctrine is that the only meaningful affirmations are those deriving from natural science. The snag, as any school student of philosophy will tell you, is that this is not itself a proposition of natural science. Whether the claim is true or false, it follows that there is at least one fact which isn't a physical fact. This was the basic lesson apparently learnt after the bubble of logical positivism burst before the Second World War.

Outgrowing God has little that is even-handed to say about the practical results of the religious enterprise, both within communities of belief and across society more broadly. It is plain that Dawkins considers faith to be a source of much more harm than good, and not just by filling people's heads with false beliefs. A dispassionate person will grant that religion can go terribly wrong on occasion. So can other forms of kinship bond, including patriotism and family life – not to mention politics. (Suppose Dawkins had announced that all left-wing endeavour is bogus in theory and ruinous in practice, because of the horrors perpetrated by Stalin, Mao and Fidel Castro. Would he be given the time of day by political scientists worth their salt?)

The other side of the picture ought to be equally evident. As well as being rich manifestations of culture, the major faiths are also vast sources of social capital and charitable outreach. Spiritually inspired conviction has mobilized millions of oppose author-itarian regimes, inaugurate democratic transitions, and support human rights. Weighing up how much harm 'religion' does relative to good is – or should be – a matter of patient sifting. Dawkins might have done better to call his book 'Outgrowing false gods'. But for that project he would have had to undertake serious research generating far fewer headlines. He would also have needed to outgrow the winner takes all mental-ity that so mars his writing in this area.

Whence all the anger, combined with tunnel vision? It is not my place to attempt a full explanation. What Dawkins does tell us is that he had a brief encounter with Christianity[22] in the form of public-school reli-gion during the 1950s, between the ages of 13 and 15, before concluding that belief in God was about as credible as trusting in the tooth fairy. Those views seem to have been set in aspic ever since. He does not reveal that he has had numerous opportunities to revisit his adolescent certainties without ever appar-ently feeling the slightest urge to do so.

Several rebuttals of *The God Delusion* have already been cited. But as far back as 1992 Dawkins debated theistic belief with John Habgood, both a professional scientist by training and then Archbishop of York. Habgood made all the points one might expect from a man of very broad range ready to see things in the round. Science is about explanation while religion centres on interpretation, he observed. God does not appear in the scientific account of nature, because the objectives and methods of science shut out anything – any hint of purpose or intention or feeling or value – which might point to a creator. That is not a criticism of science. It is a description of what science is, and the key to what makes it so successful in studying those aspects of reality in which purpose, feeling, value and so on are not part of the story. Habgood's view complements that of a Jewish leader such as Jonathan Sacks, who argues that while science takes things apart to see how they work, religion puts them together to see what they mean.[23] The right attitudes of religion to good science should always be admiration and thankfulness, Sacks adds. 'But there is more to wisdom than science. It cannot tell us why we are here or how we should live. Science masquerading as religion is as unseemly as religion masquerading as science.'[24]

It will be clear from the drift of comments made so far that *Outgrowing God* calls for further unscrambling. We must turn to this shortly. Let me end this overview on a constructive note, however. I have emphasized elsewhere the intellectual appeal of Darwinism, and my confidence that Richard Dawkins at his most constructive poses challenges to Christianity and other faiths that cannot be brushed aside casually. Look around you not only at man's inhumanity to man,[25] but also at the waste and suffering occasioned by the development of life over hundreds of millions of years, and you may indeed have questions about the biblical notion that we have a divine source and supernatural destiny. For this reason among others, I have never doubted the reasonableness of atheism. It is not unbelief as such which this book seeks to contest: only the dogmatic scorning of religious belief in principle. It is offered to the fair-minded in a spirit of openness.

2

God for grown-ups

What's in a name?

It is time to say more about how our putative creator has been conceived in the major faiths. When Richard Dawkins is not insisting that science makes the very question of God unnecessary, he is keen to remind us that deities come in many shapes and sizes. For him the variety of vegetation in the religious undergrowth is a further reason for hacking it all away. Once upon a time people gave their allegiance to Zeus or Wotan; in due course polytheism gave way to henotheism (the worship of one god in a still crowded arena) and finally monotheism as honed in a document such as Hebrew scripture. Dawkins sees biblical ideas about God as stitched from various kinds of ancient Near Eastern thread, meaning that the vision apparently does not differ in kind from those of neighbouring cultures (the Genesis creation story owes much to the Epic of Gilgamesh written in Mesopotamia, for example. Abraham may or may not have hailed from Ur, but that city boasted a civic temple to the moongod Nannar, filled with smaller shrines to smaller departmental gods for camel-drivers, cobblers and so forth). Being ignorant and superstitious, people were only ascribing phenomena they didn't understand to the antics of this or that capricious figure in the sky. No one today has any truck with Babylonian or Canaanite deities, among countless others. The modern atheist come of age simply believes in one less god. QED.

Whether this thesis is dangerous or not, it certainly shows that a little knowledge is a regrettable thing. It is also deeply unscientific. What Dawkins supposes to be a dart in the flank of his opponents is more like a boomerang. *Outgrowing God* shows no awareness at all of the markers set down by anthropologists and philosophers, let alone theologians.

Viewed from a wide angle as it has unfolded over millennia, religion is certainly very hard to define. It would include rites in the ancient world, such as animal and human sacrifice, employed as forms of scapegoating. But to focus at any length on such terrain during a brief overview would be eccentric. Anyone wanting to discredit religion today needs to confront global faiths that have produced major bodies of critical thought, and engage with definitions given by the sociology of religion, which sees its subject as involving an apprehension and symbolic representation of sacred or non-ordinary reality. Scholars in this field remind us that human beings do not merely investigate the natural world at a scientific level. We also seek to make sense of our lives via all sorts of evolutionary adaptations – agriculture, dance, literature – that have emerged from animal play, animal empathy, ritual and myth during a long history of tribal societies without much sense of the beyond, through supernatural king-god monarchies, to more recent societies with their religions of value transcending the brute givens of existence.

I have reported elsewhere a common view that some especially important developments took place during the first millennium BCE.[1] The ideal was contrasted with the real; visionary horizons of hope were set against the frustrations of the everyday world. Though expressed in different idioms across the globe, the quest for transcendence – a higher dimension of reality embodying more exalted values – arose in China, through reflection on the way of nature; in India, through worldly renunciation; in Israel, through prophetic denunciation; and in Greece, through theoretical reflection and the quest for wisdom.

Religion naturally remains an elusive term. It embraces both Sikhism and a creed without belief in God such as Buddhism. But that does not warrant the claim that *all* faiths are mutually contradictory and that if one is right, all others are wrong. Islam, for example, explicitly teaches that Christians and Jews profess significant elements of truth as 'People of the Book'. Moreover, the prologue to John's Gospel states that the Word of God enlightens all humanity.

A vital consideration is this. The major spiritual belief systems have partly inherited and partly sloughed off perspectives that were widespread in antiquity. A process of spiritual refinement is certainly discernible in the Old Testament. This evolution was not without hitches here and there. It did not unfold in a laboratory. As we have registered, a qualitative leap is nevertheless evident in a growing awareness that God is not a thing among things. The difference between monotheism and polytheism is not one of numbering, as though the issue were merely a matter of determining how many divine entities one happens to think there are. It is a distinction instead between two entirely different kinds of reality. (For more detailed statements of this case written with rigour and force, look especially at the work of a figure like David Bentley Hart.) The very division between monotheism and polytheism is in some cases a confusion of categories. Several of the religious cultures we sometimes mistakenly call polytheistic have traditionally insisted on an absolute differentiation between the one transcendent godhead from whom all being flows, and the various divine beings who indwell and govern the heavens and the earth. Only the one God, says Swami Vivekananda, speaking for much of Vedantic and Bhaktic Hinduism, is the Uncreated. The gods, though supernatural, belong among the creatures. Late Hellenistic pagan thought often drew a clear demarcation between the one transcendent God – *ho theos* (literally 'the God') – and any particular local god (*theos* without the article) who might oversee some aspect of the natural world. Dawkins begins *Outgrowing God* by explaining the etymology of 'polytheism'.[2] But he misses the one distinction in Greek that really matters in this context. Incidentally, Aquinas himself could not be clearer that God belongs to no genus. You cannot (to posit a crazy thought experiment) add up all the things in the universe, reach a figure of *n*, then conclude that the final total is *n* + 1 because you are also a theist. Divinity and creaturehood are too different even to be thought of as opposites.

We can also note that divine transcendence is pictured in broadly complementary ways across the major faiths. The conception I have in mind can be found in various forms of pagan belief deriving from late antiquity such as Neoplatonism; in the three Abrahamic religions; in Vedantic and Bhaktic Hinduism; in Sikhism; and in some aspects of both Taoism and Mahayana Buddhist visions of Buddha Nature. They all tend to see God as the one infinite source of all reality: uncreated, eternal, omnipotent, omnipresent, transcending all things and, precisely by dint of not competing for space with creation, immanent to all things as well.

The understanding of God in some traditions of Indian thought as infinite being, infinite consciousness and infinite bliss – *sat, chit* and *ananda* – is especially suggestive. It can be set alongside the Christian picture of the divine life as an eternal act of knowledge and love, and the emphasis in Sufi Islam on the shared root of the terms *wujud* (being), *wijdan* (consciousness) and *wajd* (bliss). In noting these affinities, a thinker such as Hart adds that they also connect with conceptions of religious practice found in several global faiths: 'to say that God is being, consciousness, and bliss is also to say that he is the one reality in which all our existence, knowledge and love subsist, from which they come and to which they go, and that therefore he is somehow present in even our simplest experience of the world, and is approachable by way of contemplative and moral refinement of that experience.'[3]

Even a sketch as brief as this gives us the measure not only of Dawkins's tendency to cut corners, but also of his lack of intellectual curiosity. As it happens, he does realize that some forms of Hinduism profess belief in one God behind and beyond all the others, but then makes nothing of it.[4] Now if you have been brought up assuming that Hinduism is the major polytheistic faith of the world, but then come to grasp that it is actually in some of its principal manifestations monotheistic, shouldn't that at least give you pause? Another telling point about Dawkins's opening salvo precisely concerns what he says about Zeus et al. Anyone who supposes that Greece's spiritual legacy consists mainly in tales of warring gods is wide of the mark. Out of all the great riot of classical thinking, the two figures who emerge as the greatest influences of all on Western culture are Plato and Aristotle. To see them as pagan prophets of the Christian revelation may seem like a land grab to the secularist (though it is perfectly reasonable to hold that the Church reframed some of the noblest strands in pagan thought, effectively democratizing them through an emphasis on care for the outcast). For present purposes, we might simply note that neither of these towering philosophers was a polytheist. Again, doesn't this possibly suggest that there might be more to the monotheistic instinct than first appears?

Let us turn from defensive comment to more positive visions. Ask people of faith today to give a rationale what they are doing, and – as we have seen – they are likely to reply that their beliefs need viewing in the context of life as a whole. Ritual (including symbol and gesture), narrative, ethics, institutions and personal experience all feed into the mix. Some will supplement this with observations about human nature, and what is implied by a self-examined life. Some will echo the words of Simon Conway Morris: 'The unsolved puzzle of why human beings alone among creatures have language, music, cumulative technologies, laughter, morals, teaching and, come to think of it, religions (including atheism) is the elephant in the Darwinian room.'[5] In other words, we are free, accountable and objects of judgement in our own eyes and the eyes of others. We are motivated not only by desire and appetite, but by a vision of the good. We are not just objects in a world of objects, but also subjects, relating to one another reciprocally. The philosopher Roger Scruton has summed things up with a dash of poetry: 'Our form bears ... the marks of its peculiar destiny; it is capable of sanctity and liable to desecration; and in everything it is judged by a standard not of this world.' This way of seeing ourselves does not point unavoidably towards a religious interpretation, of course. But it deploys categories that are supplied by religion, 'and to be obtained only with the greatest difficulty without it',[6] he adds.

Given the range of religious belief and practice, it may not be possible to produce an umbrella definition. But a general overview avoiding too many hostages to fortune could be that the major faiths have at their base an understanding of the onward flowing existence of the temporal world as owned and 'selved' by various kind of agent. At the centre – or one of its centres, if there is intelligent life elsewhere in the universe – stand human beings, who not only occupy existence, but are alive to it, taking it in with intelligence and giving it out with loving care. And at its top stands a creative providence of which human prudence is to be an instrument. We can connect this with Rowan Williams's definition, one of the most succinct I know. Asked once by the broadcaster Melvyn Bragg to characterize his understanding of the Almighty, he replied that 'God is first and foremost that depth around all things and beyond all things into which, when I pray, I try to sink. But God is also the activity that comes to me out of that depth, tells me I'm loved, that opens up a future for me, that offers transformations I can't imagine. Very much a mystery but also very much a presence. Very much a person.'

Something rather than nothing

We have noted the claim that only a theistic framework answers the ultimate question of why there is something rather than nothing.[7] Dawkins does not just dismiss this argument as classically stated by St Thomas Aquinas, but misinterprets it so grievously that *The God Delusion* and *Outgrowing God* invite responses on more than one level.

Known as the Five Ways, Aquinas's case requires knowledge of the Aristotelian background to be grasped in full. But it can be put in plainer terms without over-simplification. We are invited to look at the patterns and regularities of the world, and develop them to a point where we can no longer ask an intelligible question. What came before us? What do we depend on? What does *that* depend on? What came before *that*? What does *that* depend on? At some stage, according to Aquinas, we get to a point where we can no longer ask the questions What came before? or On what does this depend? We have run out of things to say in telling the story of dependence or causality. The point at which we run out of things to say and questions to ask is the moment where the language of God comes in. Not that we have reached a mathematical 'proof' of God's existence, but because we have recognized that there is something about the way we are talking that needs reframing in a larger context.

It is one measure of how shoddy a book *The God Delusion* is that its author substitutes mockery for analysis in his discussion of the Five Ways.[8] As Hart among others has pointed out,[9] Dawkins is innocent of the scholastic distinction between primary and secondary causality. (I have signposted it by the diagram on page 39.) In consequence, he thinks that Aquinas's talk of a 'first cause' refers to the initial element in a sequence of separate causes, rather than the ultimate foundation of reality. This mistake feeds another. Dawkins assumes that Aquinas's argument entails a belief that the universe had a beginning in time. This St Thomas explicitly denies. Most egregiously of all, perhaps, Dawkins thinks that the Fifth Way is a case for Intelligent Design like Paley's 500 years later, when in fact its focus is teleology or goal-directedness in nature – a subject of great interest to biologists in the modern era, as we shall see later.

Much more could be said about all this and more at a technical level. For our purposes, a pair of points stands out. One is that although some aspects of Aquinas's medieval cosmology have naturally been superseded, his core arguments are not invalidated by contemporary physics. Another scientist to miss the mark is Lawrence Krauss. His book *A Universe from Nothing*[10] – enthusiastically endorsed by Dawkins – is not really true to its title, because it assumes the existence of a quantum vacuum. And make no mistake. The quantum vacuum is none other than the physical universe at an early stage; it is replete with multi-dimensional structure and nonlinear equations of motion; it is 'about as much like nothing as a billion nuclear bombs are like nothing', in the words of a particle physicist I know. The physical chemist Peter Atkins, another Dawkins ally, proves no more convincing than Krauss in accounting for existence.[11] What Atkins calls a problem of the profoundest difficulty, namely the unfolding of absolutely nothing into something, is avoided by a claim that because the electrical charges and the angular momentums and the energies in the cosmos all add up to zero, absolutely nothing has only unfolded into nothing. Since nothing 'positive' has to be 'manufactured', there need be no 'positive, specific, munificent creation',

Atkins thinks. This is as if we argued that the Taj
Mahal does not amount to anything, because it con-
tains the same amount of stone as was quarried from
the ground to make it.

Two definitions of absolute nothingness can be
judged more rigorous. One is from the physicist Peter
Hodgson:

> Simple or complicated, small or large, the passage from
> non-existence to existence is the most radical of all
> steps. It cannot be glossed over, and no one with any
> sense of ontological reality could accept this for an
> instant. However large or small the object may be, the
> passage from non-being to being is the greatest pos-
> sible transition [and] the transition from non-being to
> being is beyond the power of science to detect.[12]

Denys Turner sums things up more succinctly still:
'"Nothing" has no process, no antecedent conditions,
no random fluctuations in a vacuum, no explanatory
law of emergence, and, there being nothing for "something" to be "out of", there can be no physics, not yet,
for there is nothing yet for physics to get an explanatory grip on.'[13]

The second point, though already outlined, needs reiterating given its fundamental importance. To grasp the classical understanding of creation both in the Abrahamic faiths and other traditions, we need to be constantly on guard against lapsing into an assumption that God is one agent among others. Expressed diagrammatically, God's causal relation to the created order would not be as the first arrow in a series of creaturely causes, but as a wholly different source: the cause or 'arrow', in Andrew Davison's analogy,[14] holding up the whole chain of creaturely causes from below:

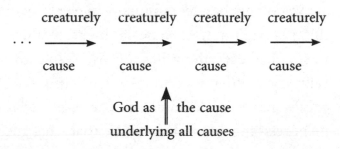

The relation of God to the world is not seen like this:

God as a	creaturely	creaturely	creaturely	creaturely
⟹ · · ·	→	→	→	→
cause	cause	cause	cause	cause

But like this:

	creaturely	creaturely	creaturely	creaturely
· · ·	→	→	→	→
	cause	cause	cause	cause

God as ↑ the cause
underlying all causes

To repeat a connected point, the case expounded by both Aquinas and his Muslim and Jewish counterparts would still hold if the universe had existed for ever. St Thomas believed that God would have been perfectly capable of creating a world that is endless in time.

A caricature of the theistic stance resurfaces from time to time. It runs like this. 'You guys are saying that there can't be an infinite regress in a series of causes, so there must be an unmoved mover at the start. But this argument for God begs two questions. First, why can't there be an infinite regress of causes; and second, if there was a first "domino" to set the chain going, who made that? You also claim that God had no cause. In that case why can't the unbeliever just retort that maybe the universe itself has no cause?'

The trouble is that major exponents of the theistic argument – Aristotle, Plotinus, Augustine and Leibniz, among others besides Aquinas – never propose anything as crude as this. None has been so callow as just to say that 'everything has a cause'. What they typically say is 'What is contingent has a cause', or 'What comes into being has a cause'. The Aristotelian argument rests in part on the premise that what goes from potential to actual has a cause. And for Aristotle, when we trace the series of things being actualized, we are kicking the can down the road. Supposing I stretch my arm. Its potential to move is actualized by signals in my brain. My brain function is enabled by molecular and atomic structure, which is in turn made possible by factors including the four fundamental forces in the universe. At each stage the explanation is deferred. From a monotheistic standpoint, it is not until you reach a reality which can actualize without itself being actualized – which is always and already fully actual, so to say – that you have an adequate explanation for existence *here and now*. Without an unmoved mover so conceived, you're left in mid-air, metaphysically. Edward Feser has likened it to placing books on a shelf, attaching that shelf to a bracket, and that bracket to a larger bracket – but somehow doing without a wall.

I am not proposing that there is no possible ground for atheism to stand on. There is, and it is given by atheists in a different intellectual league from Dawkins. J. L. Mackie is a distinguished case in point: he concluded that existence is simply a brute fact.[15] But a recourse to a brute fact can never be the outcome of an argument. It is an assumption; a claim with no other foundation than personal preference. That doesn't make it necessarily wrong, but it risks being subject to a charge of wishful thinking.

None of this is to suggest that we can give an account of God's being. Just as being aware that I exist in the world is not the same as knowing what sort of being I am, so apprehending the presence of God is a far cry from knowing what God is. Any deity sewn up in human language and categories would be an idol. But reason infers the existence of causes from the existence of effects, without always being able to stipulate the nature of the causes from the nature of the effects. If that principle holds even in mundane contexts, then it should certainly apply in a unique area of discussion such as this.

Among the more questionable moments in *Outgrowing God* comes in Chapter 12, when Dawkins says in effect that belief in a creator assumes fine-tuning in the universe, whereas atheists can accept the possibility of a multiverse. Maybe we just got lucky.[16] With this wave of the hand, he gets himself off the hook with respect to phenomena such as gravity (if it differed from its value by one part in 10^{60}, then the universe as we know it could not exist) or dark energy (forming 70 per cent of the cosmos: for the anthropic argument, this energy would have to be 'tuned' to about one part in 10^{120}). And then Dawkins moves on. Is he as rational as he thinks?

Again, there is no simple reply to this puzzle. Theists should not pretend that they have a trump card with respect to fine tuning. It is rather a fascinating part of our profound lack of understanding of major features of the world. What it means is that neither Lawrence Krauss nor any religious believer has any business being simplistic about our ultimate origins. But the theistic claim, that the world has been brought into being by a reality that is ontologically unlike it, is still reasonable. And it would stand also in the case of a multiverse. Many cosmologists with a religious faith have no theological problem with a multiverse. Why shouldn't God's creativity extend to many universes?

We have seen that Dawkins pays notoriously little attention to his critics, even when corrected on errors of fact. Faced with the above, however, he might concede that his criticisms of Aquinas were crude, but add that his instincts are democratic. My target is the simplistic world view of many ordinary believers, he might maintain.

To my mind this entails a misunderstanding of how all sorts of groups operate in practice. Divisions of labour take place across the board: non-scientists of any faith or none may agree that they accept the scientific method in principle, but leave the detail to professionals. In the same way, religious believers, while disclaiming detailed knowledge of theology, could ground their outlook in a threefold awareness – that we are embodied beings with the capacity to grasp meaning and truth; that this forms a gift prompting awe along with a heightened sense of ethical responsibility; and an acknowledgement of our status as grounded in a reality that freely bestows itself to us. As well as rehearsing other sorts of general observation outlined in Chapter 1, they would likely wish to focus on telling a story above all. Christians believe that God not only made us but also redeemed us. They therefore underline themes including freedom and divine humility: 'All praise to thee, for thou, O King divine, / didst yield the glory that of right was thine, / that in our darkened hearts thy grace might shine.' Or Charles Wesley's 'I woke, the dungeon flamed with light; / My chains fell off, my heart was free, / I rose, went forth, and followed Thee.' Jews, Muslims and others naturally have their own narratives of quest and fulfilment.

In other words, for the monotheistic traditions the reality of God is not seen primarily as a remote, offstage matter involving ultimate beginnings and ends in the grand narrative of nature, but rather an immediate and intimate presence in our responses to a call to live. The great faiths have been likened to waters shallow enough for the less well educated to paddle in, and deep enough for the cultivated to cast out into the depths. But be warned. They can also be settings for much splashing in the shallows by those who consider themselves sophisticated, while the allegedly simple-minded navigate the high seas with assurance.

Scripture and ethics

One of my favourite anecdotes about the pitfalls of translation derives from the lovely lines in Act 2 of *As You Like It*, where the Duke celebrates the Forest of Arden's many delights:

And this our life, exempt from public haunt,

Finds tongues in trees, books in the running brooks,
Sermons in stones, and good in everything.

A scholar charged with rendering the passage into German is said to have spotted a fault. 'Shakespeare must have been a bit confused. Surely what he meant to write was "sermons in books, stones in the running brooks."'

These recollections came to me as I read Dawkins on the Bible. It has become commonplace to describe him as a mirror image of the fundamentalists he has endlessly sparred with on Twitter, but the point needs restating because *Outgrowing God* is especially crude in discussing scripture. Again and again we are prompted to decide whether this or that story did or (more usually) did not take place as literally narrated. If the answer is no, Dawkins's assumption is that a whole edifice must therefore crumble. For a detailed rebuttal, I recommend the work of an expert such as Katherine Dell. The title of her book *Who Needs the Old Testament? Its enduring appeal and why the New Atheists Don't Get It* speaks for itself.[17]

So how are informed Christians to read their community's foundational text? In my book *God Is No*

Thing[18] I suggested that, rightly understood, the Bible is an extraordinary and complex human phenomenon, a library of books of every genre, evolved over centuries and held together first in Hebrew scripture by one nation's quest for identity – its account of what it means to experience God and be in covenant with him – and then in the New Testament by the ministry of an exceptional man believed by his followers to personify the Jewish nation. Fundamentalist interpretations of the Bible are not genuinely traditional: we have already noted that inspiration does not mean dictation from on high.

Genesis starts with two pictures, one of a creation recognized as good, and the other of the source of a deep fracture which spearheads the search for atonement and renewal. It leads to release from bondage, which means both freedom of a people, and deliverance from the self-absorption of sin. It includes the rejection of idols, pictured both as images of the unknowable, and the pursuit of wealth or power that we follow in denial of our real duties towards God and neighbour. The sociologist David Martin has encapsulated the significance of the New Testament as follows:

[It is about God's presence with us] as flesh of our flesh, about the proclamation of an invisible kingdom and a banquet to which we are all invited, as well as about the signs of that kingdom and that banquet, about the absorption of ... evil in the gift of body and spirit even unto death, the death of the cross, about healing of spiritual and physical wounds, the offer of a sign of peace, and the reconciliation of enmities, about rebirth, death to self and resurrection, and about the taking up of a redeemed humanity to share in the mutual exchanges of love which are the life of God.[19]

Once more, then, a Christian is not committed to belief in a specific transgression involving a snake in a garden 6,000 years ago. A literal acceptance of Genesis 1–3 has never formed part of the creed. But what the story reveals about flaws in human nature is abidingly true. A common complaint among atheists is that God is represented as vengeful in the Old Testament. I don't want to make light of this challenge – only to clarify that there is a solid answer to it. Historically, the Church has taught that a full disclosure of God's Trinitarian identity did not emerge until the life, Passion and resurrection of Christ, and the descent of the Spirit at Pentecost. In other words, the Old Testament is the first stage of an unfolding drama yet to reach its climax. It is therefore no cop-out to say that Hebrew scripture represents a genuine but partial revelation. Note that one of the first major decisions in the early Church was to abrogate the ritual elements of Jewish law.

Side by side with this should stand a general awareness about textual interpretation. It makes little sense to pluck a single leaf off a tree and pretend that it can represent an entire landscape. If one verse makes God seem cruel, for example, but the thrust of the narrative is that God's mercy exceeds divine justice, then it is the big picture that counts. Jesus himself famously summed up the whole of the Law and the Prophets in terms of radical self-giving love for God, and for neighbour defined in the broadest possible way. Nor is this approach unique to Christians. Rabbinic reflection on the Hebrew Bible displays similar impulses.[20]

This is not to suggest that textual exposition is always a smooth process. Historical analysis of the Bible, beginning in Protestant circles in the mid-nineteenth century and spreading to the Catholic world several generations later, has frequently proved challenging. But a consensus emerged. It is not an over-simplification to hold that the Synoptic Gospels (Matthew, Mark and Luke) in particular give a reliable historical account of Jesus's ministry. I especially value the outline given by a New Testament scholar such as the late A. E. Harvey: Jesus proclaimed the arrival of the Kingdom of God, 'with all that it entailed in terms of the remission of debt, the espousal of the poor and the marginalized, the casting out of evil spirits and the release of those resources of love, generosity and compassion which are so easily repressed by social convention and misguided religious scrupulosity.'[21] This mission led to Jesus's death, which he freely accepted, sensing that it would have redemptive power for the community of believers he inaugurated.

Dawkins appears unaware of this. For him either the gospels are eyewitness reportage, or the whole thing must have been a matter of Chinese whispers. He is a decidedly Protestant atheist – or rather his assumptions reflect a debased interpretation of Protestantism seeing the faith as essentially a matter of the Bible, little doctrine (apart from the atonement interpreted in one contentious way), no philosophical thought, no traditions of interpretation. But where did the New Testament come from, if not the Church? Since the canon was itself formed under the auspices of a community worshipping and reflecting together, you might suppose that the Church would possess a certain authority in proclaiming the message. The impact of Jesus's ministry was so momentous that the resulting reorganization of religious language was a centuries-long process culminating with the Nicene Creed. Just as the gospels are feeling their way towards fresh perspectives in the light of a spiritual earthquake, doctrinal formulae were 'learned, negotiated, betrayed, inched forward, discerned and risked', as one of my teachers used to put it.

Outgrowing God gives such a one-dimensional picture that questions of genre and symbol are left by the wayside. It is as if all that matters about an episode such as the Exodus is excavation of blood marks on lintel. Deliverance hardly features. Many other examples of this blind spot could be cited. Let one – the Ascension – suffice. In discussing whether the doctrine is 'true' or not, those who misinterpret it are liable to ask whether it involved vertical lift-off, as seen with the Apollo 11 rocket in 1969. St Luke tells us that he was not an eyewitness to the life of Christ.

A spiritual writer such as Erik Varden notes that the evangelist 'carefully interviews eyewitnesses, and collates their testimonies in a coherent narrative that grows in subtlety as, little by little, he comes to understand his sources better.'[22]

In Acts 1.9 (also written by Luke), we are told that Jesus 'was lifted up, and a cloud took him out of their sight'. Memo to the New Atheists: when the word 'cloud' is used in the Bible, it is unlikely to be in the context of forecasts about sunny intervals and scattered showers. A cloud was traditionally seen as a symbol of God's presence. When Israel emerged from Egypt, 'the Lord went before them in a pillar of cloud' (Exodus 13.21). God is represented as having descended to Moses in the form of a cloud on Mt Sinai. In Varden's memorable summary, the message of the Ascension is not that Christ vanishes beyond earth's orbit, but that he enters 'the Father's glory', which is set to fill the earth (Numbers 14.21) by way of preparation for the glory of eternity'.

The lesson here? To understand any sort of narrative, you need to inhabit it, sensitize yourself to its tone and terms of reference and inner harmonies. What applies to Homer, Shakespeare, George Eliot,

Mozart or any other creative artist applies all the more to that complex mixture of poetry, law, history and sermon that is the Bible. For a Catholic-minded Christian (not just a Roman Catholic), it isn't necessary to see every i dotted, and t crossed, on every page. Nor does the text offer definitive guidance on all sorts of questions that have only arisen in the modern era. What it does do is provide principles which can be applied afresh in new contexts.

What about ethics? Dawkins's reflections on the subject could hardly be more simplistic. In an extraordinary chapter on the Ten Commandments, his line of reasoning runs like this. You don't need religion and the Commandments to be good, so that blows a faith like Christianity out of the water, because it claims that you can't be good without the Ten Commandments.

This all assumes a divine-command theory of ethics divorced from natural law or virtue. One of the first lessons taught by classical tradition might say is that the Commandments are intentionally the tip of an iceberg. The goal of human life is friendship. Commandments mark out boundaries which, if crossed, indicate that friendship has been breached.

But if you thought that not lying, not committing adultery and so on got to the heart of what was going on, you would entirely miss the point. Families need house rules. Yet the idea that the essence of the family is to keep the house rules is to get the whole thing upside down.

So can a secular humanist lead a good life then? Of course. The traditional – and correct – view in Christianity is that conscience is the exercise of reasoned judgement. So natural law is just that. It is not the property of those standing in a charmed religious circle. It is less a pre-existing body of obligations and rights: more a code human beings must write themselves, using their God-given reason. Confronted with debate on matters such as abortion, cloning and euthanasia, conservatives have regularly accused politicians of 'playing God' without realizing that playing God rationally is just what the teaching of a thinker such as Aquinas demands. Natural law might be reframed as 'natural lawmaking'. St Paul in Romans 2.14 writes of how gentiles can be a law unto themselves for the reasons spelt out above. Yet none of this stops a Jew or Christian – or members of another faith groups, using their own language – from grounding ethics in the structure of reality. Religious believers can say that they are not just exercising a set of individual choices, but somehow making visible the way the world is – and ultimately the way God is. So yes, while you can lead a good life without having religious convictions, as an atheist you might have to work rather hard to explain why your moral compass isn't just arbitrary.

Perhaps the secularist might reply that Aristotle's Golden Rule is available to neutral reason on grounds already hinted at. Human beings are animals, with natural needs and capacities. The fulfilment of these needs and capacities amounts to happiness, which partly involves being honest and decent and generally doing as you would be done by. Religious voices might only be half-persuaded by this, however. What would Christians say? Since they remain Dawkins's prime targets, it seems right to focus again on church teaching, sometimes framed on the following lines. The 'cardinal' virtues of justice, temperance, prudence and fortitude are indeed rational. But it is religion that can offer the solidest grounding for the 'theological' virtues of faith, hope and charity. The Truth and Reconciliation Commission in post-apartheid

South Africa was very much an exercise of the theological virtues. I suspect that Archbishop Desmond Tutu would be among the first to say that while a secular liberal ultimately believes in justice, a Christian, also deeply committed to this virtue, nonetheless prizes forgiveness above all.

Evolution evolving

Outgrowing God is relentlessly confrontational. While discussing the book with me, a colleague suggested that the rhetorical tone is itself worthy of note. Dawkins is in effect making a declaration: 'I understand all this highfalutin science; simple-minded religious believers don't. Authority therefore resides in me. Here, for instance, is an objective account of embryology which can be contrasted with a religious view – presumably that it's all a great miracle.' In dialectical terms, Dawkins presses his 'antithesis' so hard that the unwary reader may accept the erroneous 'thesis' (namely that believers swallow a lot of bilge) from which we must apparently recoil. One result is that he is over-eager to police the notion of wonder. Feeling enraptured by the beauty of a baby, say, should not involve giving thanks to God, because we can be awestruck by the biology instead. But why does wonder need rationing in this way? It's not as if parents who have produced a second child suddenly only feel half the love they previously had for their first!

One welcome aspect of Dawkins's discussion is his chapters on emergence. Presumably he feels on especially secure ground when discussing science, even though it's precisely in his area of professional expertise that his work has drawn heavy criticism. The author first rose to prominence with his bestseller *The Selfish Gene*.[23] In this work he characterized 'memes' as mental structures that reproduce themselves – implying among other things that religion can be explained by brain chemistry. (Tell that to sociologists studying communist East Germany, one of the most secular societies on earth, and comparing it with neighbouring Poland, one of the most religious.) To talk of selfish genes, and memes, is of course to use metaphors drawn from intentional accounts of human action to describe supposedly physical processes. 'Selfish' is a highly loaded word assuming purpose, consciousness and so forth. The meme is even harder to make sense of. I don't know where Dawkins stands on memes now, but in fairness it should be noted that he regrets ever coining the 'selfish' gene idea.

My sense (shared by some of his fellow scientists speaking privately to me) is that notwithstanding a careless choice of language in the past, Dawkins was and remains reductionist in outlook. But the scientific consensus has moved on. Neo-Darwinist ideas favouring gene-centric views of biology have given way to much more holistic visions, including an acceptance of purposive behaviour.[24] Take a very distinguished physiologist such as Denis Noble, who has taught alongside Dawkins at Oxford. He was once a keen advocate of reductionism, the philosophy summarized by Jim Watson, a co-discoverer of the structure of DNA, as 'there are only molecules; everything else is sociology'. Noble saw confirmation of this view in his finding that the pacemaker function of the heart could be explained in terms of the flow of potassium and calcium ions through protein channels. Later he changed his mind, realizing that 'in the heartbeat there was not only upward causation from the molecular level to the cellular level, but also downward causation from the cell influencing the molecules.'[25] This led

Noble to reject the take on neo-Darwinism propagated by Dawkins and others for what it is – a contentious philosophical postulate, not an empirical discovery. Reductionism seeks to eliminate teleology in nature: Noble now accepts that it is ubiquitous. His recent book *Dance to the Tune of Life* maintains that genes are not agents, whether selfish or unselfish. 'There is nothing alive in the DNA molecule alone,' he writes. 'If I could completely isolate a whole genome, put it in a Petri dish with as many nutrients as we may wish, I could keep it for 10,000 years and it could do absolutely nothing other than to slowly degrade.'[26] So insofar as genes have agency, they do not have it in themselves but only as part of a complex whole – the biosphere.

Does this mean that the universe itself has an ultimate goal? Denis Noble thinks that in asking this question we reach a boundary beyond which it is not possible to go. In other words, goal-directedness does not advance the case for God. Biologists explain roots moving towards water, for example, or leaves turning towards sunlight, in terms of micromechanisms in the relevant part of the organism. More generally, any of us can understand that an organism not adapted to flourish in a given set of conditions will be eliminated, and that the struggle for survival will tend to favour the most effective teleologically configured behaviour. Fair enough. Evidence of teleology might at least bring us up short, though. The world does not just consist of meaningless bits of stuff. Matter matters; and if we believe in God on other grounds, teleology can supply an appropriate intellectual resource for conceiving God's relation to the world. We can also see why *The Origin of Species* was judged by some of its readers to be more of an aid to Christian reflection than a threat. Aubrey Moore, priest and Darwinian, provides a famous example. In the essay collection *Lux Mundi*, he spoke of Darwin's coming in the guise of a foe and doing the work of a friend. By this Moore meant that Christians could now free themselves from a deistic conception of God whereby the creator had made a machine-like world, retreated, and then occasionally intervened with a tweak. Moore believed that Darwin had restored agency to the world, while at the same time making that agency an expression of what God is. This was an echo of Aquinas's oft-quoted remark that nature is not like wood being made into a ship, but like wood that *makes itself* into a ship.

In the twentieth century, thinkers influenced by Aquinas made much of this model. Étienne Gilson noted that nature works not like the human worker assembling parts, but by producing totalities whose existence implies the existence of what we call their parts. Plants or animals are not built out of organs; organs are made in the process of producing animals and plants. So to escape a reductionist or atomistic approach, we need to see creation as dealing in whole, evolving forms, not progressing by one tiny adaptation in isolation at a time. It is now widely accepted the evolution cannot work on chance alone but that there are tendencies towards certain forms which hugely accelerate the process.[27]

These factors in turn equip us to face a vital question posed in Stephen Jay Gould's book *Wonderful Life: The Burgess Shale and the nature of history*.[28] (Burgess Shale is a fossil area in Canada showing now extinct branches of life.) Part of Gould's point is that if the remote past – and thus the lottery of life – could be re-run, then the appearance of humankind would have been extremely unlikely. Next week's weather is inherently unpredictable; what is true of the contemporary climate applies all the more to evolution over hundreds of millions of years. The Abrahamic faiths hold that the emergence of humanity was part of God's plan, but this is not to imply that God engineered the process by devising some temporal mechanism to ensure it. Nor does it make sense to think that God inserts into time from eternity some event independent of all temporal mechanisms.

A different view from Jay Gould's comes in the work of Simon Conway Morris, especially in his notion of convergence. His account deals with what might be judged more philosophically significant questions about the nature of created reality and the relation of the creature to it. He points out that the camera eye has evolved separately in very varied species (in octopuses, for example, as well as in mammals). There is something about the nature of things – see-ability or visual lucidity – that evolution explores and latches on to. Conway Morris also writes about intelligence, which has likewise evolved independently several times. That would relate to an intellectual lucidity to things, which evolution explores. The rationality of the universe affords human rationality, if you will.

Once more these considerations do not *oblige* us to think theologically. As reported, Conway Morris (Emeritus Professor of Palaeobiology at Cambridge University) is a Christian. But people of faith are usually among those most adamant that belief in God does not and cannot come at the end of an equation. What they *can do*, however, is hold up their heads and feel confident that their convictions need not be in conflict with science.

Building on this, a philosopher such as John Cottingham frames matters as follows:

Many scientists talk teleologically. It's curious, actually, that many people discussing the modern scientific world view use words like random and accidental. We're just an accidental blip on the face of the cosmos. But that can't be quite right. It does seem that it is quite natural for galaxies to form. It is natural for some stars to explode into supernovas and to produce heavier elements. It is natural for planets to form and most scientists say that, sooner or later, given the right conditions, life will emerge and then, given the Darwinian principles of selection, intelligence is likely to be favoured. So the scientific conclusion from all that seems to be that the universe is, as the British Astronomer Royal Martin Rees puts it, both biophilic and noophilic, that is to say that it will tend in due course to produce life and intelligence. There is a natural tendency there, if you like, so using words like 'accident,' 'random,' and so on is in a way misleading.[29]

Such insights tell us much. Those who see purposelessness in nature tend to impose this allegedly objective template on life as a whole. The neuro-scientist and philosopher Iain McGilchrist has recalled a wry comment of C. S. Lewis in this regard. It is like a policeman who, having himself stopped all the traffic in a certain street, should then solemnly write down in his notebook: 'The stillness in this street is highly suspicious.'

Darwin himself believed in teleology. Reviewing his legacy in the journal *Nature* in June 1874, Asa Gray wrote in terms that complement the assessment of Aubrey Moore already quoted: 'We recognise the great service rendered by Darwin to natural science by restoring teleology to it, so that instead of having morphology *against* teleology, we shall have henceforth morphology *married* to teleology.' And in response, Darwin wrote: 'What you say about teleology pleases me especially and I do not think anyone else has ever noticed the point. I have always said you were the man to hit the nail on the head.'[30] A crucial insight about Darwin seems to be this. He rejected Paley's deterministic model, whereby creation resembles a clock, but at the same time did not think that the world is the product of chance.

How might thoughtful believers standing in one of the Abrahamic traditions react to all of this? Above all by avoiding the twin pitfalls of dualism on the one hand, and materialism on the other. Dualism (often associated both with bad religion and with atheist misconceptions about what religion has to involve) asserts the pre-eminence and separateness of the mind or soul or spirit over against the body. Materialism starts with the flat, grey cosmos of the kind assumed by some neo-Darwinists. If the world consists of little lumps of stuff just rearranging my cells into different kinds of machine, then the little lumps of stuff are what is real and everything else is an assembly of them, like a bicycle or a computer. And then you have to think of consciousness and knowledge as simply by-products. So because of the way you put it together, a bicycle can transport someone; because of the way you put it together, a computer can do calculations; because of the way we are put together, consciousness emerges. But if you realize in line with modern science that matter is not little lumps of stuff but mysterious patterns of interaction located in space and developing through time, then you will be a bit more ready to think with Aristotle, let alone Aquinas, that what really exists are whole beings. The whole life of a dog or a cat depends on, but subsumes into a bigger whole, the complex interactions of electrons in the molecules and cells of the animal, and so on. And once you are amazed at the powers of animals to organize and interpret and react to their sense data, then you are on your way to seeing humans as higher beings still, with a power to integrate their judgements at an intellectual level.

The modern world finds it especially hard to reckon with a divine creator because of our machine-dominated paradigms. Newton unravelled some of the machinery of the heavens; other scientists did the same for the earth; Darwin began to unravel the machine of life; now practitioners of AI promise to unravel the machinery of the mind. All this has served to dethrone God as designer and engineer. But organisms are not machines. Their insides are similar, but not their outsides. Despite their internal organization, organisms implement no external function. Organs do, but organisms don't. You can ask what eyes are for, but not what dolphins are for.

A friend who had taught both science and theology once remarked to me that organisms differ from machines not in their works but in the quality of their idleness. Just as clocks can't tell the time, the one thing machines built to be light-sensitive cannot do is see. They can respond appropriately to different colours and so forth, *as if* they were seeing. That is not vision, however. Yet if machines can be made to work like organisms, you might reply, then it is possible to manufacture everything that matters. What is left out is superfluous. 'Exactly so!' my friend added. 'When you are trying to grasp how sight works, the actual seeing is an entirely idle component. Nevertheless I value that idle experience as I value life itself: it precisely gives colour to my life, awakes in me the feeling of being alive within a living world I am in touch with and inhabit.' He went on to suggest that considerations such as these enabled him to see God 'on the surface of things'. On reflection it strikes me as fitting that people of faith should find traces of the divine on this level, as well as in the depths.

To sum up: I am not convinced that Aquinas's Fifth Way (concerned with goal-directedness) works as an absolute proof. But if on the basis of an argument such as the Third Way – which in part rests on wonder over why there is anything at all – you grant that God holds everything in being, then you can see that part of the beauty and truth of what God has made is this whole flourishing of living things. The process is indeed thrown up by evolution. But the theist can add that things flourish and achieve their goals following the patterns that all come ultimately from God who sustains everything – things and their patterns – in existence.

So it is not necessary or even desirable to take the Fifth Way as a good standalone demonstration of a creator. If you do believe in God, though, then it points to something exciting, which is that God doesn't just push things. From the deistic argument of the seventeenth century, we have inherited a sense already described of God as a watchmaker or engineer who manufactures the cosmos, gives it a shove, and on it rumbles. From time to time theology has lent credence to this idea. That makes you want to defend the spontaneity of living beings, and especially the freedom of human persons, as if these qualities had to be championed over against the creator. Yet the Fifth Way, and the importance of final causality in Aquinas generally, makes us think of God as attracting processes to their fulfilment – drawing out rather than pushing. For many believers, that gives a much more attractive and gentle and intimate picture of divine action.

A brief closing thought. In writing about science in this book, I have not found it particularly difficult to identify professional biologists who made significant contributions to their discipline in the modern period, and did so coming from a theistic perspective. In the scientific body as a whole they form a minority, but an intelligent and significant minority. In Richard Dawkins's output, by contrast, another picture of science is given – that it is essentially atheistic. Is Dawkins's picture a fair representation, an admissible estimate, or is it unbalanced and therefore misleading? The evidence suggests that people of faith have contributed sufficiently well to mainstream biology to make the picture painted by Dawkins unbalanced. He has therefore misled his readers, both in *The God Delusion* and *Outgrowing God*. But on the religious side there is also much unbalanced and misleading material coming from various sources at the conservative end of the spectrum. So a good number of people of varying outlooks need to put their houses in order. The main point is simply that Darwin's theory is not a 'dangerous idea', as Daniel Dennett and others would like us to believe. It is unthreatening and, indeed, welcome to theism as long as we step back and consider deeply what it does and does not imply.

3

Live and let live

D oes Richard Dawkins even agree with himself? Among other pieces of evidence I have in mind is an article he wrote for *The Guardian* in 2002 extolling a spirit of free enquiry in the classroom.[1] Despite a welcome side-swipe against the teaching of creationism at a school in Gateshead, Dawkins's focus was not on religion. Volleys were instead directed at the rigid, box-ticking culture beloved of some educationalists.

The heart of the piece was a tribute to F. W. Sanderson, headmaster of Dawkins's school, Oundle, from 1892 to 1922. Sanderson's faith was yoked to a passion for science: the subject became part of the core curriculum on his watch. Dawkins judged that Sanderson's sermons in the school chapel could reach 'Churchillian heights', quoting one such address celebrating great pioneers:

Mighty men of science and mighty deeds. A Newton who binds the universe together in uniform law; Lagrange, Laplace, Leibniz with their wondrous mathematical harmonies; Coulomb measuring out electricity... Faraday, Ohm, Ampère, Joule, Maxwell, Hertz, Röntgen; and in another branch of science, Cavendish, Davy, Dalton, Dewar; and in another, Darwin, Mendel, Pasteur, Lister, Sir Ronald Ross. All these and many others, and some whose names have no memorial, form a great host of heroes, an army of soldiers – fit companions of those of whom the poets have sung...

As well as taking the complementarity of science and religion for granted, Sanderson nursed a healthy contempt for jingoism. Another of his addresses juxtaposed the Sermon on the Mount with the unthinking patriotism attached to Empire Day ('Blessed are they that mourn, for they shall be comforted. Rule, Britannia! Blessed are the meek, for they shall inherit the earth. Rule, Britannia!'). He also did away with what he saw as undue institutional restrictions, even asking that laboratories be left open at all times to let pupils pursue their own projects. He died suddenly in 1922 having just given a lecture, chaired by H. G.

Wells, to science teachers gathered at University College London. Speaking in the same place and to a similar audience 80 years later (this time presided over by an 'enlightened clergyman'), Dawkins reported hearing of deep worries among today's teachers about a failure to teach evolution in British schools. The blame for this lay not with faith groups, but with the A level syllabus itself. 'Evolution gets only a tiny mention, and then only at the end of the A level course. This is preposterous for, as one of the teachers said to me, quoting the great biologist Theodosius Dobzhansky (a devout Christian, like Sanderson), "Nothing in biology makes sense except in the light of evolution."'[2]

Though of a different generation from Dawkins, I sat in the same lab as him decades later and was inspired by the same biology master, Ioan Thomas – also spoken of with great respect and affection in *The Guardian* piece cited and, as it happens, also a person of strong Christian conviction. (When I left the school it was to spend a while teaching in the state sector, and finding proof of the adage that good and less good teaching styles cut right across all sorts of other divides.)

Anecdotes like these could be greatly multiplied and serve several purposes. Again and again, angry atheists link religion in general and Christianity in particular not just to multiple falsehoods but to mind control. Two logically separate points are being conflated. First stand questions about the credibility of this or that article of faith. Then there is the issue of whether young people inducted into a particular tradition – Christian, humanist, Buddhist, you name it – are allowed to make up their own minds about it and move on if they wish.

Anyone who feels indignation over Christianity's role in promoting ills from social repressiveness to imperialism is wholly right about something. Believers and atheists alike can deplore the Church's record – and their arguments will naturally carry all the more conviction if balanced by an awareness of faith-inspired efforts to promote goods including the rule of law and democracy, as well as science. If your inner jury is still out on this, consider an advocate such as Tom Holland, author of *Dominion: The Making of the Western Mind*.[3] Far from being a static force, Holland shows, Christianity has repeatedly discharged 'pulses of energy that rip up society'. Belief that human beings are made in the image of God, that the poor, widows and orphans should have first claim on our attention, that our creator should be pictured as much as a humble servant as a mighty judge: all these have subverted and remade one society after another.

This view coheres with that of another historian, Larry Siedentop, who holds that roots of liberalism were established in the arguments of philosophers and canon lawyers by the fourteenth and early fifteenth centuries:

> belief in a fundamental equality of status as the proper basis for a legal system; belief that enforcing moral conduct is a contradiction in terms; a defence of individual liberty, through the assertion of fundamental 'natural' rights; and, finally, the conclusion that only a representative form of government is appropriate for a society resting on the assumption of moral equality.[4]

Closer to our own day, the Jewish jurist René Cassin, and Hansa Mehta, the Hindu feminist campaigner, were heavily involved alongside Christians in drafting the UN Declaration of Human Rights. This document eschews confessional language in the interests of

maximizing consensus, but the theological background is easily recognizable. Shun this background,
say its defenders, and what emerges is either an over-
mighty state on the one hand, or the tyranny of economic neoliberalism on the other. Christian
resources can offer much to promote debate and
positive action, especially over environmental steward-
ship and climate change.[5] Over the past century the
Catholic Church has done more than any other insti-
tution to demonstrate the abiding relevance of biblical and classical principles of justice and charity.
Despite massive failings in other areas, its records on
Third World debt, conscientious consumption habits,
the environment, and socially responsible uses of tech-
nology speak for themselves. An inventory of related
examples covering other churches and faiths would
fill many stout volumes.

This is especially important given the so-called
return of religion today. In the words of two distinguished sociologists, Monica Duffy Toft and Timothy
Samuel Shah, 'The belief that outbreaks of politicized
religion are temporary detours on the road to secu-
larization was plausible in 1976, 1986, or even 1996.
Today, the argument is untenable. As a framework for

explaining and predicting the course of global politics, secularism is increasingly unsound. God is winning in global politics. And modernization, democratization and globalization have only made him stronger."[6] Although Christianity has been in retreat across Europe for more than a century, three-quarters of the world's current population professes a faith. That figure is due to reach the 80 per cent mark by 2050.

We hear much about the perils of fundamentalism – Christian and Hindu, as well as Muslim. Though partly understandable, this is also a function of the journalistic thirst for bad news. A volcanic eruption will make the front pages; channels supplying irrigation and stability to entire regions over extended periods will not. Pentecostalism is in many ways the Christian counterpart of Islamic revivalism, but remains largely ignored by the Western media because it is resolutely non-violent. This counts as a great oversight. The added value supplied by good religion for development in the Global South is immense. In and around the megacities of Latin America, Africa and Asia stand many thousands of Pentecostal communities, often led by women, in which people are (among much else) getting their lives on track and supporting those poorer than themselves. A thumbnail sketch such as this should not ignore China. As recently as the 1970s, religion had notionally been eliminated from the world's most populous society. Market reforms were not just introduced to catch up with the West from the 80s onwards. Aware of a moral vacuum, the Communist Party allowed spirituality to re-emerge, without realizing that religion might come back to haunt the powers that be in the form of anti-corruption campaigns. Civil society is likely to develop in fits and starts across China in decades to come. The speed of the process will have much to do with a religious revival of unprecedented scale.

Analogous considerations apply to Islam. I have mentioned that it is fair to point up the menace posed by Islamist extremism (and equally fair to acknowledge that today's jihadists have learnt their deadly craft from secular ideologies such as Leninism). But defence voices can be drowned out by the case for the prosecution. The late Shahab Ahmed's important book *What Is Islam?*[7] traces an immensely rich cultural genealogy in what the author terms the Balkans to Bengal strand of the faith: tolerant, undogmatic, hospitable to science and other forms of secular learning.

The instability in a good number of Muslim-majority countries today is certainly theological to a degree (though again, Islamic fundamentalism remains a largely modern reform movement insecurely rooted in classical thought). It is also geopolitical. Interfaith tensions along or near the tenth parallel of latitude north of the equator merge with ethnic conflict, along with battles for land, water and oil. Understanding when and to what extent religion features is a complex matter. Slogans, of course, are the province of the ignorant or the incautious.

We are once more coming to the undramatic conclusion that life is in practice a good deal messier than dogmatists of all persuasions would have us believe. Richard Dawkins, Christopher Hitchens, Philip Pullman and other godless standard-bearers avoid argumentative subtlety through an identification of evil with religion as such. So the 'proof' that faith causes violence is seen as a simple matter of identifying 'facts' such as the Crusades. Once more, little or no effort is made to lay bare the social structures through which religion is filtered. Pullman's linking of evil with 'the Authority' (religion in light fictional disguise) is even more revealing. The vision grows

from a large seam of politics which proclaims inno-
cence and pins all that is toxic on a particular structure – capitalism or patriarchy, say – which must be
eliminated. It would be much fairer to argue that on
the whole, religion is associated with war when it gets
fused with the nation and the state, which manage
the use of force. Faith then becomes one more facet
of group identity to be mobilized in a conflict.

So banning religion (to cite a battle-cry of the artists
Gilbert and George) – as well as being deeply author-
itarian, of course – is unlikely to transport us to the
sunlit uplands imagined by some secularists. Just look
at what has happened in societies from Egypt and
Turkey to India and Indonesia after an earlier generation of elites imposed secularism from on high. Religion
of a more carnivorous form, often tinged with nation-
alism, has resurfaced. Rather than sidelining faith, gov-
ernments would be well advised to allow it a voice in
the public square. Not to dominate, but to be a respect-
ed part of the argument about the social good.

This should not be seen as a matter of pragmatism
alone. Secular libertarian blueprints for the good life
often appear thin. There is little to say beyond talk of
the freedom to do what we like and buy what we can

afford. Religion is perhaps especially well placed to confront the problems associated with material advance and moral decay. The economic and social changes that promised human emancipation have also created the conditions for its debasement into empty commodity culture and narcissism. Is secularism able to frame a sufficiently robust counter-narrative through its own resources alone? Many who doubt it can be forgiven their scepticism.

No surprise, then, that acute voices see abiding force in older, largely faith-based traditions speaking of solidarity, justice, compassion and the non-negotiable dignity of human life. Jonathan Sacks puts the matter with typical aplomb in his book *The Dignity of Difference*: 'The sheer tenacity of the great faiths – so much longer-lived than political systems and ideologies – suggest that they speak to something enduring in human character. Above all, it was religion that first taught human beings to look beyond the city-state, the tribe and the nation to humanity as a whole. The world faiths are global phenomena whose reach is broader and in some respects deeper than the nation-state.'[8]

One of the best attempts to ford these choppy waters in more recent times has come in Rowan Williams's distinction between good and bad models of secularism: the 'procedural' and the 'programmatic'. I have reported this argument elsewhere, but it bears repeating. Procedural secularism grants no special privileges to any particular religious grouping, but denies that faith is merely a matter of private conviction. Larger visions should be allowed to nourish the public conversation. Williams sees so-called programmatic secularism in a far less positive light, because it insists on a 'neutral' public arena and hives religion off into a purely private domain. Rather than resolving clashes of outlook, programmatic secularism risks inflaming social conflict by stoking resentment among faith groups. Williams's recipe for harmony is 'interactive pluralism', which encourages robust dialogue among faith communities and between them and the State. No one has received the whole truth 'as God sees it', so all have something to learn.

From this it is possible to see religion as a bulwark against a potentially over-mighty state – the state in which liberalism has become a substantive programme, rather than a force for defending genuine diversity and the freedom of conscience. We could benefit from dusting down a definition of liberty produced by Lord Acton in the 1870s. For him, the liberal state does not have a moral agenda except the preservation of the liberty of all its constituent communities. In that sense respect for freedom of belief is or should be the first mark of a liberal state, just as political liberty should underpin the health of faith groups.

Insights underlying this argument are transposed into a secular key by a French thinker such as Alain Finkielkraut. He is as wary of the authoritarian Right as of the utopian Left. Noting an 'ethnocentrism of the present' seen as no less narrow-minded than old-style jingoism, he deplores a climate in which school pupils are encouraged to rewrite classic texts as Facebook entries. 'What is gloriously described as openness to life is nothing more than the closing of the present on itself,' he writes in his book *L'identité malheureuse*. An implication of this is that the very idea of superior wisdom, whether of teachers or ancestors, is doubted or jettisoned. 'All authority is questioned, except that of public opinion.' As the commentator Henri Astier has noted,[9] Finkielkraut stands in a tradition chronicled by the historian Antoine Compagnon in his book *Les antimodernes*.

'Anti-moderns' are not reactionaries: they don't pine for the past, but simply have bracing views on the inadequacies of the present.

It doesn't seem too much of a stretch to see a connection between Finkielkraut's jeremiads about society and Dawkins's on education – and a further correspondence between both and thoughtful faith-based contributions to the debate. Readers of Gibbon will recall his remark in *The Decline and Fall of the Roman Empire* about how sacred rituals were viewed: as true by the ignorant masses, as false by the philosophers and, by the magistrates, as a convenient means of social control. Some may suspect me of variations on the magistrate's theme. But no. It is respectable to argue that religion has its origins in scepticism rather than credulity, because our ancestors thought it jejune to imagine that reality consists only in what we can see. At moments of acute intemperance Dawkins has gone so far as to equate religious instruction with child abuse. (He has also taken some people aback by adding that children should know their Bibles, and lamenting the ignorance of young people about stories and characters that ought to be part of our cultural furniture.) A more level-headed treatment of this area would encompass the horrors of atheist fundamentalism, as well as its religious form. Dawkins is right about the dangers of certainty: but the greatest bloodbaths in history have been caused not by the dogmas of religion, but those of pseudo-science. Think of Nazism and Communism, ideologies both claiming scientific certainty rooted in race and historical sociology respectively.

Richard Dawkins's latest book is stimulating at times, but colossally frustrating overall. It conflates Zeus, Frejya, Brahma and the God of Jesus Christ right up to its final page. It ends with this avuncular question: 'I think we should take our courage in both hands. Grow up and give up on all gods. Don't you?' I can only answer with a quizzical shake of the head. Courage to be an atheist? Where? You certainly need courage to renounce religion in parts of the Islamic world today, and in some parts of America. You also need courage to embrace a faith in societies including China. In the West as a whole, though, unbelief is manifestly the default setting. Yet I reply in the negative to Dawkins's question not to encourage you into the opposite camp necessarily: we should all follow our lights while doing our best to keep them in good working order. With respect to religion as well as so much else, that means evaluating the real deal, not a grotesque caricature. And since this is a supremely an area in which grown-ups can disagree in good conscience, it also entails respect for the other. Should that really need pointing out?

Perhaps Coleridge saw furthest and best in Aphorism IX of his *Aids to Reflection*: 'In Wonder all Philosophy began; in Wonder it ends: and Admiration fills up the interspace. But the first Wonder is the offspring of Ignorance: the last is the parent of Adoration.' These words have been given a contemporary lilt by Mark Vernon, a figure commanding respect not only for his record as a public intellectual with qualifications in physics and philosophy, but also because he was once an Anglican priest. He resigned from the ministry after losing his faith, but later began to doubt his doubts. *Pace* Richard Dawkins, intellectual liberation is not a one-way street. I commend the review Vernon wrote of *The God Delusion*: though searing, it is also constructive.[10] There is a 'clear link' between science and religion, Vernon has argued in another context:

though deploying different discourses, both can be expressions of the uncertainties of the intellect, and yield intimations as to what lies beyond. They are manifestations of what the Renaissance humanist Nicholas of Cusa called 'learned ignorance'. He, in turn, was recalling Socrates' great insight, that the key to wisdom is not how much you know but is having some understanding of the limits of your knowledge. Moreover, a keener appreciation of such limits is part and parcel of the increase of knowledge, as contemporary physics shows when its greatest discoveries simultaneously throw up increasingly profound conundrums, such as the anthropic coincidences and why there is something at all...

...the nub of the issue is the fundamentalist mindset, manifest in the individual – secular or religious – who refuses to accept the ambiguities of existence and the ethical weight of wonder.'[11]

Notes

1 A dialogue of the deaf

1   As suggested at the outset of my book *God Is No Thing: Coherent Christianity* (Hurst, 2016), any claim about the apparent marginalisation of religious belief is likely to draw a hollow laugh in some quarters. Public religious voices in North America and parts of Europe are often robust and sometimes shrill. In the UK, of course, Church and State are still officially connected, even if the cords that bind them have been slackening for over 150 years. Perhaps it is precisely these factors which render dislike of Christianity in particular all the more pointed, however – especially among opinion-formers. A few random examples confirm a broader pattern. In the supposedly subversive minstrels' gallery of our culture, 'rebellion' can be no more than trite orthodoxy. The comedian Frank Skinner, who returned to the Church a few years ago, has quipped that to succeed in his trade you need to 'wear skinny jeans, have hair like a chrysanthemum, and be an atheist'. In a BBC interview, the painter and printmaker Anthony Green declared that a focus on religious themes can be the kiss of death to an artist's career. Discussing Marilynne Robinson's acclaimed novels *Gilead, Home* and *Lila*, the journalist Bryan Appleyard has written that these works will seem curious to a high number of readers, 'because what is going on here is religion'. He went on to argue that 'many, probably most, British people – artists, writers, audiences – will find this exotic because to them, religion has been embarrassed out of existence.'

2   Richard Dawkins, *The God Delusion* (Black Swan, 2006), pp. 180ff.

3   For a notable example of this misguided approach, see Steve Jones, *The Serpent's Promise: The Bible Retold as Science* (Little, Brown, 2013).

4 Francis Spufford, *Unapologetic: Why, despite everything, Christianity can still make surprising emotional sense* (Faber, 2012), p. 102.

5 Denis Alexander, reviewing Jerry Coyne, *Faith vs Fact: Why Science and Religion are Incompatible, The Times Literary Supplement* (*TLS*), 23 January 2016, <www.the-tls.co.uk>.

6 Ronald Numbers (ed), *Galileo Goes to Jail: And other Myths About Science and Religion* (Harvard University Press, 2009). Incidentally, fewer than half the scholars contributing to this volume are religious believers.

7 See Richard Dawkins, Daniel Dennett, Sam Harris and Christopher Hitchens, *The Four Horsemen: The Discussion that Sparked an Atheist Revolution* (Bantam, 2019).

8 Richard Dawkins, *Outgrowing God: A Beginner's Guide to Atheism* (Bantam, 2019).

9 Christopher Hitchens, *God Is Not Great: How Religion Poisons Everything* (Atlantic, 2007).

10 Sam Harris, *The End of Faith: Religion, Terror and the Future of Reason* (Free Press, 2006).

11 Daniel Dennett, *Breaking the Spell: Religion as a Natural Phenomenon* (Penguin, 2006).

12 Stephen Fry, in *The Four Horsemen* (Bantam, 2019), p. xiii.

13 Alister McGrath, *The Dawkins Delusion? Atheist Fundamentalism and the Denial of the Divine* (SPCK, 2007). See also among other examples, John Polkinghorne, *Science and Religion in Quest of Truth* (Yale University Press, 2011), Janet Martin Soskice, *The Kindness of God: Metaphor, Gender and Religious Language* (Oxford University Press, 2008) and Keith Ward, *The God Conclusion: God and the Western Philosophical Tradition* (DLT, 2009).

14 David Bentley Hart, *Atheist Delusions: The Christian Revolution and its Fashionable Enemies* (Yale University Press, 2009).

15 Edward Feser, *The Last Superstition: A Refutation of the New Atheism* (St Augustine's Press, 2008).

16 Denys Turner, *Thomas Aquinas: A Portrait* (Yale University Press, 2013), p. 106.

17 Terry Eagleton, reviewing Dawkins, *The God Delusion*, in *The London Review of Books*, 19 October 2006 <www.lrb.co.uk>.

18 Anthony Kenny, reviewing Feser, *The Last Superstition*, TLS, 22 July 2011 <www.the-tls.co.uk>.

19 John Gray, *Seven Kinds of Atheism* (Allen Lane, 2018).

20 Giovanni Tiso, *New Humanist* (Summer 2019), pp. 30–33 <www.newhumanist.org.uk>.

21 *Ibid.*

22 A press release reproduced on the title page of *Outgrowing God* reveals that the author abandoned all religious belief at the age of 15.

23 Jonathan Sacks, 'Even great science tells us nothing about God', *The Times* (3 September, 2010) <www.thetimes.co.uk>.

24 *Ibid.*

25 As well as focusing unduly on weaker anti-theistic arguments, Dawkins makes curiously little of what in my view is by far the strongest argument against faith in a benign, all-powerful providence, namely the problem of evil and suffering. The challenge was expressed with particular force by David Hume, himself paraphrasing Epicurus. 'Is God willing to prevent evil, but not able? Then he is not omnipotent. Is he able, but not willing? Then he is malevolent. Is he both able and willing? Then whence cometh evil? Is he neither able nor willing? Then why call him God?' I do not believe that this deepest of conundrums for the believer can be fully or tidily resolved. Since Dawkins underplays it, however, I will confine myself to saying that I attempt an answer from a Christian perspective in *God Is No Thing* (pp. 87–91) and that the most searching brief book on the subject I have yet encountered is David Bentley Hart's *The Doors of the Sea: Where Was God in the Tsunami?* (Eerdmans, 2005). Aquinas's view, highly influential in Western Christianity, is that not even divine omnipotence can create a finite world in which natural evils will not be a concomitant of good. Allowing sin is an inevitable consequence of allowing freedom. But this is only an initial move. The terrain in

question is always moral and existential. It cannot be circum-vented by logic. What faith offers is not a demonstrative or even probabilistic solution to the amount of suffering in the world, but a resolve never to abandon the path of love.

2 God for grown-ups

1 Rupert Shortt, *Does Religion Do More Harm than Good?* (SPCK, 2019), pp. 11–12.

2 Dawkins, *Outgrowing God*, p. 4.

3 David Bentley Hart, *The Experience of God: Being, Consciousness, Bliss* (Yale University Press, 2013), p. 44.

4 Dawkins, *Outgrowing God*, p. 9.

5 Simon Conway Morris, reviewing A. N. Wilson, *Charles Darwin: Victorian Mythmaker*, in *The Tablet*, 7 September 2017 <www.thetablet.co.uk>.

6 Roger Scruton, *Gentle Regrets: Thoughts from a Life* (Continuum, 2005), pp. 226–7.

7 For an especially interesting discussion by a philosopher willing to follow the argument where it led, see Antony Flew with Roy Abraham Varghese, *There Is a God: How the World's Most Notorious Atheist Changed his Mind* (HarperOne, 2007).

8 Dawkins, *The God Delusion* pp. 100–103.

9 Bentley Hart, *The Experience of God*, pp. 333–4, n.1.

10 Lawrence Krauss, *A Universe from Nothing: Why There is Something Rather than Nothing* (Simon and Schuster, 2012).

11 Peter Atkins, *On Being: A Scientist's Exploration of the Great Questions of Existence* (Oxford University Press, 2011).

12 Peter E. Hodgson, *Theology and Modern Physics* (Routledge, 2005), p. 193.

13 Turner, *Thomas Aquinas: A Portrait*, p. 142.

14 Andrew Davison, 'Looking Back Toward the Origin: Scientific Cosmology as Creation *ex nihilo* Considered "From the Inside"', in Gary. A Anderson and Markus Bockmuehl (eds), *Creation ex nihilo: Origins, Development, Contemporary Challenges* (Notre

Dame University Press, 2018), pp. 367–82. See also his gloss on Hodgson, p. 388: 'It is even beyond the power of science to theorize this 'transition', and the inexplicability of this 'transition' relates precisely to the point that it is not a transition: creation is not any kind of change...'

15 See J. L. Mackie, *The Miracle of Theism: Arguments For and Against the Existence of God* (Oxford University Press, 1983).

16 Dawkins, *Outgrowing God*, pp. 270ff.

17 Katherine Dell, *Who Needs the Old Testament? Its Enduring Appeal and Why the New Atheists Don't Get It* (SPCK, 2017).

18 Shortt, *God Is No Thing*, pp. 74–80.

19 David Martin, reviewing A. C. Grayling, *The Good Book: A Secular Bible*, *TLS*, 3 June 2011 <www.the-tls.co.uk>.

20 It is well established that the Rabbis of the Talmud (and afterwards) used creative methods to negate laws in the Bible which they felt subverted the broader narrative. A favourite technique was to put a non-literal interpretation on the law. In the case of the injunction to kill the Amalekites in 1 Samuel 15, for example, the Rabbis said that when Sennacherib invaded Palestine he mixed up all the nations of the area so that it was impossible to know who was an Amalekite; therefore the law, albeit not revoked, could no longer be applied (among other Talmudic references, see *Berachot* 28a).

21 Andrew Chandler (ed), *The Terrible Alternative: Christian Martyrdom in the Twentieth Century* (Cassell, 1998), p. 4.

22 Erik Varden, *The Tablet*, 25 May 2019 <www.thetablet.co.uk>.

23 Richard Dawkins, *The Selfish Gene* (Oxford University Press, Oxford: 1976).

24 Denis Noble, 'Why Replace Neo-Darwinism?' in *The Dance Sourcebook* <http://www.musicoflife.website/pdfs/The%20Dance%20Sourcebook.pdf>.

25 For a discussion of Noble's ideas aimed at non-specialists, see Anthony Kenny, *An Illustrated Brief History of Philosophy* (Wiley-Blackwell, 2018), pp. 409ff.

26 An even more lucid overview can be found in the section on Denis Noble in Anthony Kenny, *Brief Encounters: Notes from a Philosopher's Diary* (SPCK, 2018).

27 See especially Iain McGilchrist, *The Master and His Emissary: The Divided Brain and the Making of the Western World* (Yale University Press, 2009; new edition, 2019). Also Addy Pross, *What Is Life: How Chemistry Becomes Biology* (Oxford University Press, 2016).

28 Stephen Jay Gould, *Wonderful Life: The Burgess Shale and the Nature of History* (Norton, 1989).

29 John Cottingham, *Philosophy and Theology* 24(1) (2012), pp. 85–111.

30 É. Gilson, trans. J. Lyon, *From Aristotle to Darwin and Back Again: A Journey in Final Causality, Species and Evolution* (Ignatius Press, 2009), p. 100.

3 Live and let live

1 Richard Dawkins, 'The Joy of Living Dangerously' (*The Guardian*, 6 July 2002) <www.theguardian.co.uk>.

2 *Ibid.*

3 Tom Holland, *Dominion: The Making of the Western Mind* (Little, Brown, London: 2019).

4 Larry Siedentop, *Inventing the Individual: The Origins of Western Liberalism* (Allen Lane, 2014), p. 332. For an especially illuminating discussion of this passage, and a refutation of Steven Pinker's neglect of Christianity's role in fomenting progress, see Nick Spencer, <https://www.theosthinktank.co.uk/comment/2018/02/20/enlightenment-and-progress-or-why-steven-pinker-is-wrong>.

5 Pope Francis, *Laudato Si: On Care for Our Common Home* (CTS, 2015).

6 Timothy Samuel Shah and Monica Duffy Toft, 'Why God Is Winning', *Foreign Policy*, 9 June 2006 <www.foreignpolicy.com>.

7 Shahab Ahmed, *What Is Islam?: The Importance of Being Islamic* (Princeton University Press, 2015).

8 Jonathan Sacks, *The Dignity of Difference: How to Avoid the Clash*

of Civilizations (Bloomsbury, London: 2002), Introduction.

9 Alain Finkielkraut, *L'identité malheureuse* (Stock, Eugene, OR: 2013); translated by Henri Astier, *TLS*, 1 August 2014) <www.the-tls.co.uk>.
10 Mark Vernon, <https://philosophynow.org/issues/62/The_God_Delusion_by_Richard_Dawkins>.
11 Mark Vernon, reviewing John Loftus, *Why I Became an Atheist, TLS*, 2 April 2010, <www.the-tls.co.uk>.

Suggestions for further reading

Justin Brierley, *Unbelievable?: Why After Ten Years of Talking with Atheists, I'm Still a Christian* (SPCK, 2017)

Tim Crane, *The Meaning of Belief: Religion from an Atheist's Point of View* (Harvard University Press, 2017)

Edward Feser, *Aquinas: A Beginner's Guide* (Oneworld, 2009)

David Bentley Hart, *Atheist Delusions: The Christian Revolution and its Fashionable Enemies* (Yale University Press, 2010); and *The Doors of the Sea: Where Was God in the Tsunami?* (Eerdmans, 2011)

J. L. Mackie, *The Miracle of Theism: Arguments for and Against the Existence of God* (Oxford University Press, 1983)

Sara Maitland, *Awesome God: Creation, Commitment and Joy* (SPCK, 2002)

Herbert McCabe, *God Matters* (Mowbray, 2006)

Alister McGrath and Joanna Collicutt McGrath, *The Dawkins Delusion?: Atheist Fundamentalism and the Denial of the Divine* (SPCK, 2007)

Iain McGilchrist: *The Master and His Emissary: The Divided Brain and the Making of the Western World* (Yale University Press, 2019)

Malcolm Murray, *The Atheist's Primer* (Broadview, 2009)

Malise Ruthven, *Islam: A Very Short Introduction* (Oxford University Press, 2012)

Jonathan Sacks, *The Great Partnership: God, Science and the Search for Meaning* (Hodder, 2012)

Nick Spencer, *The Evolution of the West: How Christianity Has Shaped Our Values* (SPCK, 2016)

Francis Spufford: *Unapologetic: Why, Despite Everything, Christianity Can Still Make Surprising Emotional Sense* (Faber, 2013)

Index

Index